See No Evil,
Hear No Evil,
SMELL
NO EVIL

by Anna Jane Hays   pictures by Joe Mathieu

A SESAME STREET/GOLDEN PRESS BOOK

Published by Western Publishing Company, Inc.,
in conjunction with Children's Television Workshop.

Copyright © 1975 Children's Television Workshop
MUPPET characters © 1971, 1972, 1973, 1975 Muppets, Inc.
All rights reserved. Printed in U.S.A.
Sesame Street and the Sesame Street sign are
trademarks and service marks of Children's Television Workshop.
GOLDEN, A GOLDEN SCRATCH AND SNIFF BOOK, and GOLDEN PRESS®
are trademarks of Western Publishing Company, Inc.
The "Microfragrance"™ labels were supplied by 3M Company.
Library of Congress Catalog Card Number: 72-2885